LIFE IN TUDOR TIMES

BY
JOHN GUY

COUNTRY LIFE

HOME BREW

Most country households brewed their own wine, beer or cider. Any left over was taken to nearby towns in barrels on packhorses.

While poorer people still farmed strips of land in large, open fields and paid a tythe, or rent, to the Church or local lord who owned the land, a new type of farmer was emerging, called yeomen. They rented or bought several fields together to form small farms, usually on the outskirts of the village, and built themselves fine houses. They also employed labourers from the village to tend the fields instead of working on the land themselves, and formed a 'middle class' of landowner, not as wealthy as the lords but much better off than the peasants.

WORKING THE LAND

Despite the growth of towns in both size and number, about 90 percent of the population still earned their living from the land.

NATURAL CYCLES

Country life was ruled by natural cycles; by the seasons, the weather and the number of daylight hours. Certain tasks had to be performed at certain times of the year. Here, peasants are pruning vines, usually done each March.

OFF TO MARKET

Most towns held a weekly market, where people from the surrounding villages came to sell their goods and buy any goods not available locally. Poultry, butter, eggs, cheese, grain, fish and livestock were all sold at markets. Like fairs, they became great social gatherings.

DOMESTIC COMFORTS

Life in the countryside was simple, but standards of living were improving as the country as a whole began to feel the benefits of increased foreign trade and travel. The quality of houses improved and higher wages meant that more people could eat more healthily. Some could now afford meat and vegetables to add variety to their basic diets. This picture shows a fish and sausage being grilled. The picture on the right is a leather water bucket.

VILLAGE LIFE

Village life had changed little since the Middle Ages. Most people did not travel far from home. Villages had their own windmill to grind corn, and local tradesmen made and sold goods not produced by the villagers themselves.

LIFE IN TOWNS

Improved methods of agriculture meant that fewer people were needed to work the land. Many peasants were removed from their homes when their fields were sold off or turned over to sheep pasture for the rapidly growing wool trade. Most people moved into towns to find work as labourers for the growing number of merchants and traders who set up business there as a result of increased foreign trade.

These changes happened fairly quickly which meant overcrowding was a problem. Many of the houses were of poor quality and crammed into narrow streets. There were frequent outbreaks of disease, such as plague and cholera.

FRESH WATER

Fresh drinking water in towns was difficult to find. Most people bought their supplies from water-carriers, who brought water in from the country.

Following the introduction of coffee into England from South America it quickly became a very fashionable, though expensive drink. Rich people met at 'coffee houses' in towns to exchange ideas and read newspapers (introduced in 1622 but only available in limited editions) or political pamphlets.

FIRE

One of the biggest risks in towns was fire. Most of the buildings were made of wood and thatch, so the flames to spread easily. The Great Fire of London started on 2 September 1666. It raged for five days killing nine people and destroying over 13,000 buildings.

LIFE FOR THE RICH

B y contrast, many people already comfortably off became very wealthy indeed, mostly as a result of increased foreign trade as England began to extend its empire. With a strong government at home, many nobles replaced their drafty, old castles with modern mansions. They also spent vast amounts of money on clothes and jewellery.

HEAVY ARMOUR

Although changing methods of warfare had made armour outdated, many noblemen still owned a suit of elaborately decorated ceremonial armour, which they might wear at court or, as in this case, at their own funeral.

A COVER UP

To hide the often unpleasant smells found around the house, or town, wealthy Tudor women carried a pomander, or scent bottle, on their belt. This example dates from c.1580 and had four separate compartments for different perfumes.

A LOVE TOKEN

Miniature portraits were painted for husbands and wives from wealthy families to be inserted in jewellery, such as this gold locket (c.1590), and carried as a love token.

OLD BEFORE THEIR TIME

This painting of the Saltonstall family shows clearly the fashion for wealthy parents to dress children as young adults as soon as they were out of baby clothes.

HOME COMFORTS

Furniture in wealthy Tudor households became ever more elaborate and comfortable, as shown by this exquisitely carved four-poster bed. Curtains could be lowered for privacy and warmth.

ART FOR ART'S SAKE

With the opening up of the seaways in the 16th and 17th centuries great fortunes were made, allowing the rich to adorn their houses with works of art. This 'Nautilus Cup' (c.1585) is made of silver gilt and shell.

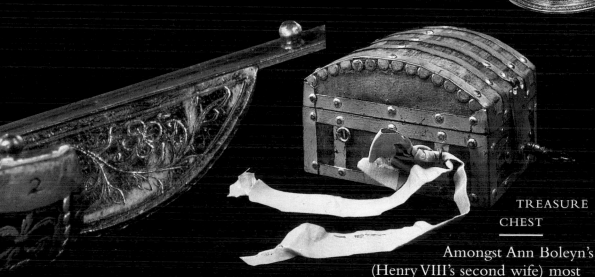

TREASURE CHEST

Amongst Ann Boleyn's (Henry VIII's second wife) most treasured possessions was her jewellery, which she carried with her on her frequent royal processions in this charming casket.

THE POOR AT HOME

*T*t is estimated that in the 16th and 17th centuries about half the population were poor. Many had to beg, although it was illegal and they might be punished, or even hanged, if caught. Eventually, almshouses were set up to help the poor, elderly and ill who could no longer support themselves.

TRADITIONAL ROLES

Traditionally, all men and women in the poorer households had to work and had their own duties. The roles were clear – the men working mostly in the fields and tending the livestock, while the women did the housework, cooked and made clothes. At busy times, such as harvesting, women would also be expected to help their husbands on the land.

SIMPLE LIVING

The poor often had a simple standard of living. Many still farmed the strips of land on the outskirts of the villages and kept a few chickens to improve their income by selling the eggs. The husband and wife in this illustration are chasing away a fox that was about to kill one of their chickens.

ARE YOU SITTING COMFORTABLY ?

Furniture was basic in poor households, usually consisting of a trestle table and bench seats. The roasted pig in the middle of the table indicates this is a special occasion.

MEALTIMES

Only the well-off could afford pewter tableware, the poor had to make do with earthenware, often made by the householders themselves. This clay jug is typical and dates from about 1550–1600.

IN THE NURSERY

One of the main duties for women in the poorer households was looking after the children. Here, a mother is seen nursing a baby, with an older child beside her.

A WOMAN'S WORK

Women also carried out dairy tasks, including the production of butter and cheese. Traditionally, they took their own produce to market and were allowed to keep the money to spend as they wished.

FOOD AND DRINK

The rich ate well, with a wide variety of meats and vegetables regularly on the menu, including potatoes, recently introduced from America but still very expensive. Poorer classes had a more basic diet of dairy produce, bread, basic vegetables and occasionally meat, such as rabbit. The rich drank wine at table, while the poor drank ale. Food was preserved in spices, or salt, though there were experiments with ice as a preservative by the late 17th century.

DELICACY?

While we might frown upon it now, swans were considered a great delicacy for the rich. Poorer classes would be happy with goose though.

FOOD DISPENSER

This fine piece of tableware is a Tudor peppermill recovered from the *Mary Rose.*

TABLE SERVICE

These dishes and plates are of pewter or wood and are typical examples of tableware from early Tudor times. They were found in the wreck of the *Mary Rose.*

TABLE MANNERS

The children of Lord Cobham seated around the table are eating a variety of fresh fruits – with their pets wandering amongst the food!

HARE TODAY, GAME TOMORROW

Hare and game birds, such as pheasant or partridge, were food for the rich man's table, while rabbits, caught wild, might be part of the poor man's diet.

FOOD PREPARATION

The kitchen at Hampton Court shows how food was prepared (usually on wooden surfaces) in the 16th and 17th centuries. Cooking was still done mostly on open fires.

'GIN LANE'

Alcohol was cheap and the poor began to drink very heavily. This became a problem, as this engraving by Hogarth shows.

IMPROVING THE FLAVOUR

To improve the flavour of game, such as pheasant, deer and rabbit, it was hung in a cold room for several days before eating. This is still done today, but in the 16th and 17th centuries meat was left until maggot-ridden to sweeten the taste.

PASTIMES

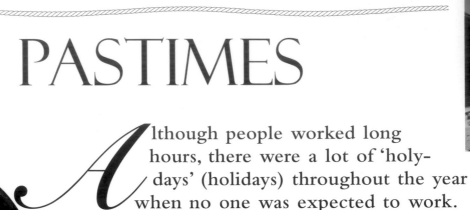

Although people worked long hours, there were a lot of 'holy-days' (holidays) throughout the year when no one was expected to work. People played a variety of games (for fun rather than as organized sports) such as hockey, cricket and football. Football was played with a pig's bladder for a ball, and was very different from today's game. Two teams from neighbouring villages met somewhere between the two communities. The object was to get the ball back to your own village – any way you could! The theatre was popular, though women were not allowed to act, so young boys took women's roles.

HITTING THE RIGHT NOTE

For people of all classes music has always played an important role as a source of entertainment. The Tudor period saw the growth of individuals learning to play an instrument, or singing, for their own amusement.

TREADING THE BOARDS

This picture shows the reconstructed open-air Globe Theatre. The original was built in 1598-9 and was the most popular theatre in London. William Shakespeare owned an eighth share in it and staged many of his plays there.

THE BARD OF AVON

William Shakespeare (1564-1616) is perhaps the best-known and greatest English dramatist. He began his career as a stage hand in the Elizabethan theatre, then as an actor, before going on to write plays.

THE HUNT

Hawking and hunting remained popular pastimes throughout the Tudor period. Deer were the most popular, but wild boar and wolves still roamed the countryside then and were hunted, too.

BLOOD SPORTS

Bear-baiting, where dogs were set upon a captive bear and bets made on the outcome, was a popular though cruel blood sport.

BOARD GAMES

Board games were popular indoor pastimes. This backgammon board (known as tables) was found aboard the *Mary Rose*.

COMING UP TRUMPS

Card games were popular, both for pleasure and for gambling. The four players here are playing primero, an early sort of poker. The modern card pack is still based on Elizabethan court dress.

FASHION

ashion trends were greatly influenced by the monarch and court. The rich spent a lot of money on clothes. Elizabeth I had 260 gowns, 99 robes, 127 cloaks, 125 petticoats and hundreds of smaller accessories in her wardrobe. For the poor, coarse woollen clothes had to do, dyed one colour using vegetable dyes. But for the rich a range of materials was available, including linen and silk, which could be dyed or printed in a variety of colours and often richly embroidered. Women wore loose ruffs, while men strutted about wearing huge, padded shoulders.

LUCKY CHARM

Pendants, such as this one worn by Elizabeth I, were believed to ward off evil and ill-health.

LAYER UPON LAYER

Clothes for men were built up in layers for extra warmth. The nobleman in this picture wears leggings beneath a short tunic, with an inner and an outer cloak of ermine-lined red velvet.

FINE JEWELS

Both men and women wore beautiful jewellery. Many fine jewels were imported with the opening of new trade routes, such as this late-medieval necklace from Russia.

THE VIRGIN QUEEN (1558-1603)

Elizabeth I, daughter of Henry VIII by his second wife, Ann Boleyn, was very particular about her appearance and is said to have taken a bath (then considered unhealthy) four times a year, whether she needed it or not!

BLACK TEETH

Many Tudor people had rotten teeth. However, one of the more unusual fashions of the time was the practice of deliberately blacking-out the front teeth, particularly among noble women. This may have developed to disguise genuinely rotten teeth.

IF YOU CAN'T STAND THE HEAT

To disguise the pock scars of smallpox, candle wax was smoothed into the skin. The wax tended to melt if it came too close to the fire!

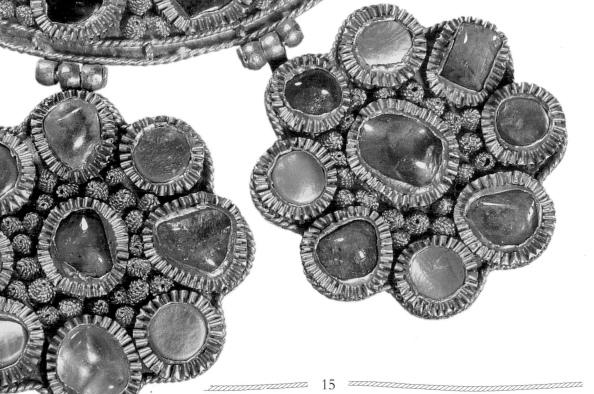

ART AND ARCHITECTURE

Great houses were usually built in brick, making them warmer and much more welcoming than the stone medieval houses had been. More attention was also given to comfort, and large windows to let in extra light. Poorer people used white plaster between the blackened wooden timbers of the walls of their houses, creating the distinctive black and white style we recognize today. The use of coal for fuel became widespread, and because coal produces more smoke than wood, chimneys became a common feature of houses for the first time.

SUMPTUOUS INTERIORS

Without the constant threat of war, money could be spent on the interior comforts of castles and houses.

CHANGING STYLES

Ightham Mote, an unfortified manor house in Kent, shows a delightful blend of medieval and Tudor features.

RED-BRICK MANSION

Originally begun in 1515 by Cardinal Wolsey and given to Henry VIII, Hampton Court has been greatly extended by successive monarchs. It is a magnificent, beautifully decorated palace with no defensive features.

THE AMBASSADORS

This is one of many paintings that Hans Holbein the Younger produced at the court of Henry VIII. This painting is unusual because at the bottom is a skull, which can only be seen properly from the side.

FURNITURE AS ART

This elaborately carved case is made from imported black ebony wood. Each panel contains a miniature painting and bust.

EVERY PICTURE TELLS A STORY

Portraits became popular under the Tudors. This study of Edward VI, by an unknown artist, is typical of the period. Tudor artists tried to capture the expression of feeling. By contrast with medieval paintings, which were more symbolic, Tudor works are more natural and try to flatter their subjects.

HEALTH AND MEDICINE

CRUEL TO BE KIND

Although it looks like he is being tortured, this patient is having a brain operation, without an anaesthetic.

There were frequent outbreaks of bubonic plague. The culprit was a species of flea, carried by rats aboard ships coming from the Middle East. Nearly 80,000 people died in England in the 1563 outbreak alone. Diseases, especially epidemics such as plague or cholera, were seen as punishment from God, and magical remedies were still in any treatment to rid the patient of evil. It was widely believed that illnesses were caused by 'bad blood', and so bleeding was seen as an effective cure for many diseases. Sometimes this meant using leeches to suck blood from the patient.

ST BARTHOLOMEW'S HOSPITAL

This hospital was first founded in 1123, but Henry VIII refounded it in December 1546. He provided it with land and properties, and granted it to the City of London. The main gate to the hospital has a statue of Henry VIII above the door.

BUBONIC PLAGUE

At the time of the plague, no one knew what caused it. Plague doctors wore beaked masks filled with herbs and spices, which they hoped would protect them from infection. One of the early symptoms of the plague was sneezing – death usually followed within just five days. A handbell (below) was rung by the undertakers who collected the dead.

A MODERN EVIL

Although Sir John Hawkins introduced tobacco into England (from the American colonies in 1565), it was Sir Walter Raleigh who made smoking fashionable. Today about one in four smokers dies from diseases directly caused by smoking, but at that time nobody knew the dangers.

LIFE EXPECTANCY

This picture shows the five ages of man - baby, youth, adult, old age and finally death. Child mortality was high, over half of those born died in their first year. Only one person in ten was expected to reach 40.

LOVE AND MARRIAGE

For most people marriage was more a matter of convenience than love. Many noblemen arranged the marriages of their children (particularly girls, who might be married as young as 12) for political or financial reasons. For the poorer classes it was often simply a matter of girls looking for any man who might be able to support them.

VOWS OF CHASTITY

Everyone entering into marriage took vows of chastity (to be faithful to each other), but some husbands, particularly lords away at court, took them very seriously indeed. They made their wives wear a chastity belt to make sure they remained faithful.

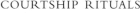

COURTSHIP RITUALS

Young suitors of noble birth called upon their ladies at court (from where the modern word courtship derives) and conducted their romances under the supervision of chaperones.

MARRIAGE FEAST

This painting of a marriage feast at Bermondsey about 1569 gives a good impression of an Elizabethan society wedding. Festivities could go on for several days.

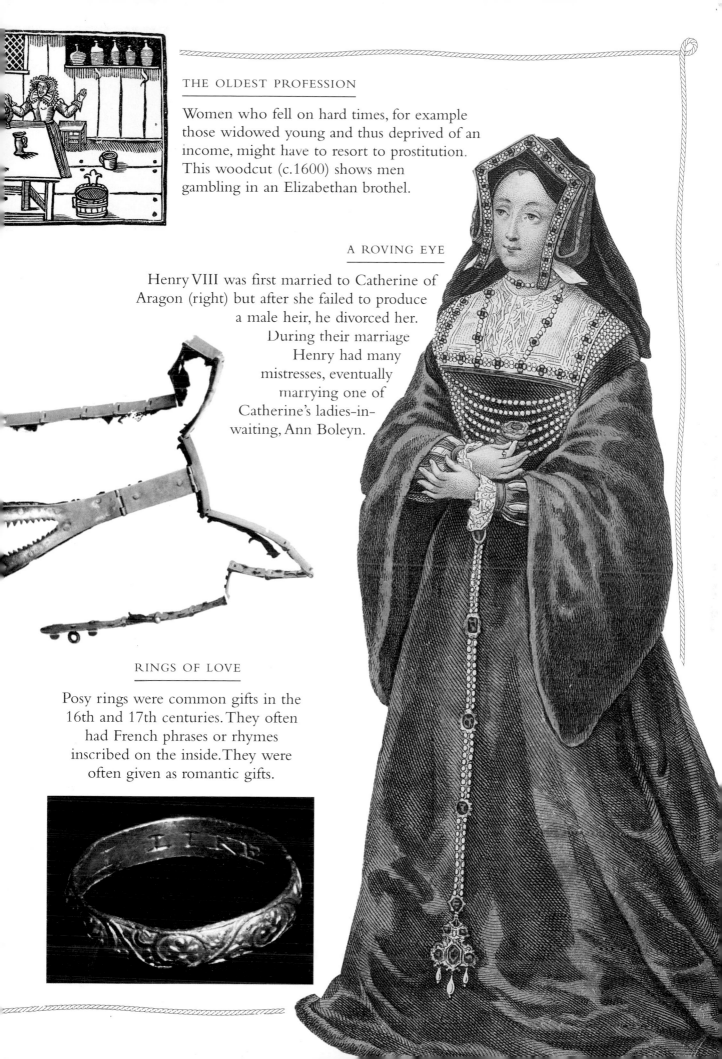

THE OLDEST PROFESSION

Women who fell on hard times, for example those widowed young and thus deprived of an income, might have to resort to prostitution. This woodcut (c.1600) shows men gambling in an Elizabethan brothel.

A ROVING EYE

Henry VIII was first married to Catherine of Aragon (right) but after she failed to produce a male heir, he divorced her. During their marriage Henry had many mistresses, eventually marrying one of Catherine's ladies-in-waiting, Ann Boleyn.

RINGS OF LOVE

Posy rings were common gifts in the 16th and 17th centuries. They often had French phrases or rhymes inscribed on the inside. They were often given as romantic gifts.

WOMEN AND CHILDREN

Tudor England was very much a male-dominated society in which women and children had few rights. Wives were expected to obey their husbands and if they did not, or if they nagged, they might face the ducking stool as a punishment. Women were expected to help out in the fields, cook, keep house and mind the children. The only real profession open to them was nursing. Only children from wealthy families went to school, and then usually just the boys.

CHILD'S PLAY

Although poorer children started work as young as six to help support the family, there was also time to play. This toy gun is made of wood.

HORN BOOK

Children were taught to read using a simple horn book. A piece of paper, mounted on a wooden board, was covered by a thin sheet of transparent horn as protection.

ALL IN A DAY'S WORK

This cottage interior shows a mother and grandmother carrying out cooking and laundry duties, while a child learns to walk in a wheeled baby walker.

FUN AND GAMES

The boys in this picture (from a well-off family judging by the clothes) are playing a form of hop-scotch.

'BLOODY' MARY

Although Princess Mary was the first of Henry VIII's children to survive, women had few rights and succession to the throne was considered unseemly. She only succeeded to the throne following the death of Edward VI, her half-brother. She was a Catholic and had over 300 people executed for refusing to revert to Catholicism.

A WOMAN'S LOT

Midwifery was one of the few professions open to women. Note the surgical instruments on the belt of the seated woman. The men in the background are calculating the astrological chart for the new baby.

ORPHANS

Orphaned children had no rights whatsoever. For the lucky ones special courts appointed guardians, but many lived on the streets, relying on Church charity for food.

A TRAGIC AFFAIR

Lady Jane Grey was the cousin and childhood sweetheart of Edward VI. When he realized he was dying, he decided that she should rule after his death instead of his half-sister, Mary. She came to the throne at 16 and ruled for just nine days, before giving up the crown to Mary. She was later beheaded for treason.

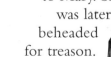
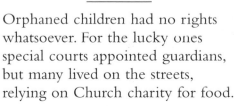

WAR AND WEAPONS

The Wars of the Roses were civil wars between the rival families of York and Lancaster, each claiming the English throne. Richard III lost his crown to Henry Tudor (House of Lancaster), who as Henry VII became the first Tudor monarch in 1485. When Henry VIII split with the Church of Rome he angered the Pope and lived under constant threat of invasion. Relations with Spain worsened in Elizabeth's reign when a massive armada was sent against England in 1588, which was defeated by Sir Francis Drake, amongst others.

MONS MEG

This bombard weighing over 8 tonnes, could fire a stone cannon ball nearly three kilometres.

FIRE IN THE NIGHT

On 28 July 1588, eight fireships were set alight and cast by the English amongst the Spanish Armada in Calais. The Spanish captains panicked and set out to sea. This broke their formation and was the turning point in this naval battle.

KEEPING UP APPEARANCES

By the 16th century, with the development of guns, fighting armour was light, often consisting of breastplates and helmets only. Armour, such as this suit, was more ceremonial than practical, used mostly for tournaments.

YEOMEN OF THE GUARD

Following Henry VII's victory at Bosworth Field in 1485 several attempts were made on his life. As a precaution, he established a personal bodyguard unit of yeomen at the Tower of London. Their successors still wear the same scarlet uniforms today.

THE ROUTE OF THE ARMADA

Following their famous defeat in August 1588 the Spanish Armada took flight northwards, around the coast of Scotland. Of 130 ships, only 70 returned home to Spain.

LINES OF DEFENCE

Deal Castle, Kent, as it appeared when newly completed in 1540. The largest of the Henrician (meaning, 'of Henry's reign) coastal forts, it was also the most powerful, defended by cannons and handguns.

CRIME AND PUNISHMENT

FLOGGING

Flogging was a common punishment for a number of minor offences, such as stealing, or even simply being caught begging.

The increased trade and improved farming methods, as well as making some people rich, also created a crime wave among those could not find work. The population rose, but fewer people were needed to work the land. Many landlords turned peasants out of their homes, turning their fields and common lands into sheep pasture. It is estimated that by 1560 there were more than 10,000 homeless people wandering the countryside looking for work. Many started begging, while others turned to crime, even though harsh punishments had been introduced.

HENRY VIII'S IRON RULE

When Henry VIII divorced his first wife, Catherine of Aragon, and broke from the Church of Rome, there was the constant threat of rebellion. He ruled the land with an iron fist and is thought to have executed several thousand people (though no accurate records exist) mostly because of their religious or political beliefs.

ROYAL PRIVILEGE

Royal prisoners who had been condemned to death, reserved the right to be beheaded by an executioner using a sword, instead of an axe, as it was considered more dignified. Ann Boleyn chose this method for her execution in 1536.

A SENSE OF JUSTICE

Taxation was high and punishments severe. Most towns had a court where Justices of the Peace, travelling the land, heard criminal cases, but they were unpaid and therefore could be bribed.

OFF WITH THEIR HEADS

The block and axe was usually reserved for nobility and political prisoners for crimes against the Crown. Victims knelt before the block, with arms stretched, but the axe was not usually sharp enough to cut off the head with one blow.

DEATH BY STONING

Adulterers, or those committing crimes against the Church, were sometimes executed by stoning, or by crushing, having heavy stones piled onto their chests.

TRANSPORT AND SCIENCE

Travel was very difficult, and dangerous, throughout the Tudor period. Some of the main roads had metalled surfaces, but most were little more than beaten earth, which became very muddy and impassable in winter months. Most people walked or went on horseback because carriages were still very uncomfortable. In towns, the rich were conveyed in Sedan chairs – similar to a small carriage but with handrails instead of wheels – carried by two men.

In 1543 the astronomer Nicolaus Copernicus published a radical new theory: that the Earth and other planets went around the sun. This challenged the belief that the Earth was the centre of the Universe. His ideas were rejected by the Catholic Church, and not generally accepted until many years later.

HEARTS OF OAK

English shipbuilders became world leaders in designing ships to carry cannon, helping sailors such as Drake, Raleigh and Frobisher to rule the seas. Many ships were built at the royal dockyards of Chatham and Woolich, where there were plenty of trees. The oak forests of Kent and Sussex were managed carefully to provide a supply of timber.

HIDDEN WORLDS

With the invention of the microscope, scientists could see tiny creatures and organisms, such as this flea, scarcely visible to the human eye, for the first time in dazzling detail.

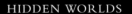

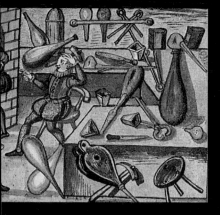

THE SORCERER'S APPRENTICE

Alchemists believed they could turn ordinary metals into gold. They were not successful but they advanced the study of chemistry, especially in medicine.

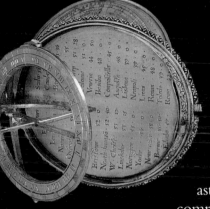

IT'S IN THE STARS

Instruments such as this brass astronomical compendium, made in 1569, were used for accurate navigation. They were also used to make astrological charts, which were taken very seriously.

MICROSCOPIC DETAIL

This 17th century compound microscope is similar to one used by the eminent physicist Robert Hooke. For the first time, microscopic creatures, too small to be seen with the human eye, could be observed.

DAWNING OF A NEW AGE

This atmospheric engine, used to pump water from mines, was developed by Newcomen and dates from 1705.

RELIGION

The 16th century was a period of great upheaval and reform in the Church. There was already a growing number of people who objected (Protestants) to the Catholic faith before Henry VIII's break with Rome. When Henry failed to get a divorce from Catherine of Aragon from the Pope, he set up a separate Church of England with himself as head. The Protestants welcomed the new Church, which eventually became accepted as a Protestant faith.

CHURCH REFORMS

Pilgrimages to religious shrines were outlawed by the 17th century church reformers who stripped them from the churches.

PURITAN REFORMS

Following the Reformation of the Church by the Tudors, most church decoration, such as this colourful triptych (altar piece) was removed by the Puritans. They wanted to simplify worship and were against lavish artworks and religious symbols.

A FAIR TRIAL?

Anyone accused of witchcraft was ducked under water. If they drowned, they were considered innocent, but if they survived they were deemed to be a witch and then executed!

DISSOLUTION OF THE MONASTERIES

Henry VIII accused the monasteries of corruption. He closed them down between 1536 and 1540, taking their wealth for himself.

THE REFORMATION

In 1533 Parliament passed the Act of Appeals, asserting England's independence from Rome. The following year the Act of Supremacy made Henry 'Supreme Head of the Church of England'.

CARDINAL WOLSEY
(1475–1530)

Cardinal Wolsey enjoyed a rapid rise to fame and fortune as Henry VIII's Lord Chancellor. But he fell out of royal favour when he failed to get Henry's divorce from Catherine of Aragon. He was arrested and ordered to the Tower of London for trial, but died on the way.

THE BOOK OF COMMON PRAYER

This Catholic missal was replaced by the first English Book of Common Prayer in 1549, following Henry VIII's break with the Church of Rome.

GLOSSARY

Almshouses Specially built houses or buildings for poor people to live in. They were charities and came from the Church tradition of giving aid to the poor.

Anaesthetic Something that reduces a person's ability to feel pain. Before this was invented, all operations were carried out with the patient wide awake.

Armada A fleet of warships. The Spanish Armada was a naval invasion planned by King Philip II of Spain against England.

Astrology The study of the stars and planets and how they are thought to affect human behaviour and events.

Cholera A serious infectious disease which effects the intestines. It is caused by eating or drinking something infected with the bacteria.

Ducking stool A chair or stool on the end of a long pole. It was used to dunk people into ponds or rivers as punishment.

Midwife A person specially trained to help women when they give birth.

Pruning Cutting away dead or overgrown branches from trees and plants. This helps the plant grow.

Tythe Paying 10 percent of your income to the Church or government.

We would like to thank: Graham Rich, Rosie Hankin and Elizabeth Wiggans for their assistance.
Copyright © 2008 *ticktock* Entertainment Ltd,
Published in Great Britain by *ticktock* Media Ltd.,Unit 2, Orchard Business Centre North Farm Road, Tunbridge Wells, Kent TN2 3XF, U.K.
All rights reserved. No part of this publication may be reproduced, stored in a retrieval system, or transmitted in any form or by any means electronic, mechanical, photocopying, recording or otherwise, without prior written permission of the copyright owner.
A CIP catalogue record for this book is available from the British Library.
ISBN 978 1 84696 654 5
Picture research by Image Select.
Printed in China.